Heffers of Ca  KU-165-276

Bookshop   20 Trinity Street (Tel. 58351)

A large and exciting bookshop : come and see it. We sell books new, secondhand and paperback in many languages and covering all fields : from cookery books to linguistics, from current novels to the sciences and oriental studies. Our mail order service extends all over the world. Catalogues are free on request. And we welcome browsers. Open Monday to Saturday, 9.00-5.30.

Children's Bookshop   27 Trinity Street (Tel. 56200)

A bright modern bookshop selling the best books for children. Open Monday to Saturday, 9.00-5.30.

Paperback Shop   13 Trinity Street (Tel. 61815)

A first-class range of paperbacks. Open for eleven hours each day, Monday to Saturday, 9.00-8.00.

Penguin Bookshop   51 Trumpington Street (Tel. 58351)

An attractive shop devoted entirely to Penguin books. Open Monday to Saturday, 9.00-5.30.

Stationery Shop & Art Gallery   19 Sidney Street (Tel. 58241)

Four floors, served by a lift, selling pens and stationery, current literature and children's books, office equipment and typewriters, gifts and pictures. An art gallery above the top floor holds regular exhibitions. Open Monday to Saturday, 8.45-5.30.

Artists' Shop   21 King Street (Tel. 58241)

A complete range of materials for professional and amateur artists. Open Monday to Saturday, 8.45-5.30.

Drawing Office Centre   26 King Street (Tel. 58241)

A shop with a specialist range of technical drawing equipment. Open Monday to Saturday, 8.45-5.30.

Heffers Printers Limited   King's Hedges Road (Tel. 51571)

A Bookshop in Britain

with customers all over the world

We have sold books for almost a hundred years. From our headquarters at 20 Trinity Street, Cambridge, we send books of every kind to universities, libraries and other institutions throughout the world – and, of course, to private customers. Our tradition of personal, expert service to all who use and love books is continued from our superb new bookshop opened in 1970. Orders and enquiries by post receive prompt and knowledgeable attention. Visitors to the bookshop are most welcome.

Ordering Books

At 20 Trinity Street we carry an extensive stock of new and secondhand books in all subjects. Orders for titles not on our shelves are placed with publishers, and the books sent to our customers as soon as they are received in Cambridge. Any book available anywhere in the world can be supplied to order. We will search on request for secondhand copies of books no longer in print.

Account Facilities

We offer credit account facilities to anyone who will spend over £10 a year in our shops. An application form to open an account is available. Payment for books is simple: we have arrangements with banks in many countries.

Catalogue Mailing List

Account customers throughout the world are invited to join our mailing list and to receive attractive free catalogues in their fields of interest.

For further details of our services please write to

W. Heffer & Sons Ltd
20 Trinity Street
Cambridge England

Telephone Cambridge 58351

Pitt Building
Trumpington Street

The first University Printer set up his Press in 1521. Today **Cambridge University Press** *publishes Bibles and Prayer Books, works of scholarship, university text books, schoolbooks and learned journals.*

Heffers
Stationery Shop
and Art Gallery
19 Sidney Street

Telephone Cambridge 58241

Ground Floor

Personal and college stationery, printed and die-stamped notepaper, and engraved visiting cards. Pens and ball pens, albums, leather goods and souvenirs of Cambridge. Notebooks, files, University and school stationery supplies. British and foreign maps and guide books. Diaries.

First Floor

Books: general literature, children's books, paperbacks. Bibles and Prayer Books. Greeting cards for all occasions.

Second Floor

Commercial stationery, loose-leaf ledgers, charting systems. Typewriters, adding, dictating and copying machines. Electronic calculators. Filing cabinets, desks, tables and chairs.

Third Floor

Handcrafts and games for all ages, children's art supplies. Original paintings, lithographs, engravings, framed and unframed reproductions. British Museum replicas, picture framing and photograph frames.

The Heffer Gallery

Exhibitions throughout the year.

illustrated guide
to Cambridge

Clare College: the Bridge and the west front, with King's College
Chapel in the background

illustrated guide to Cambridge

with a map of the Colleges and City centre

by FREDERICK BRITTAIN, Litt.D.

based on the Guide by Frank Rutter
first published in 1922

FIFTEENTH EDITION
fully revised and reset

W. Heffer & Sons Ltd
Cambridge

Fourth Impression © Mrs M. Brittain 1974   ISBN 0 85270 017 2

Printed in England by Heffers Printers Limited, Cambridge

Contents

A **bold** letter after an entry refers to a square on the folding map of central Cambridge at the end of this Guide. An *italic* letter appears after a building or place beyond the area of the map, and refers to the square showing the road to be taken to reach it.

Contents

Illustrations

Illustrations

The drawing of the Gate of Honour, Gonville and Caius College, on the front cover is by Rodney Shackell.

The aerial view of Cambridge on page 16 is reproduced with permission from a photograph by J. K. St Joseph, Cambridge University Collection, Copyright Reserved.

The photograph of the Fitzwilliam Museum on page 32 is reproduced by permission of the Syndics of the Fitzwilliam Museum, Cambridge.

Rupert Brooke's photograph on page 90 is printed by courtesy of Messrs Faber and Faber, publishers of Christopher Hassall's biography *Rupert Brooke* in which it appears. We are indebted to Mr John Schroder, owner of the negative, for supplying a print of the photograph and for giving us permission to reproduce it.

Prints of the photographs by Edward Leigh reproduced in this Guide are obtainable from him at 22 Derby Road, Cambridge.

General Information

The Colleges are usually open to visitors during daylight hours, but they must keep off the grass, must not take in dogs, push-chairs or other vehicles, and must not smoke.

COLLEGE CHAPEL CHORAL SERVICES

For vacation services enquire at porters' lodges.

King's College. Sunday, 10.30, 3.30. Weekdays, 5.30. Open on weekdays, 9–4; in vacation, weekdays, 9–6; Sundays, 10.30–6.

Trinity College. Sunday, 9 and 6.15, in full term. Choral Evensong: Wednesday, 6.30. The Chapel is open all day.

St John's College. Sunday, 10.30, 6.30. Weekdays (except Monday), Saints' Days and Eves, 6.30. Open 10–12, 2–4.

Jesus College. Choral Evensong: Tuesday, Thursday, 6.55; Saturday, 6.45; Sunday, 6.30. The Outer Chapel is open all day.

MUSEUMS

Fitzwilliam Museum. Admission free, weekdays, 10–5, Sundays 2.15–5. The Museum is closed on Good Friday, Christmas Day and Boxing Day.

Kettle's Yard (Northampton Street). Collection of modern paintings and sculpture: daily in term, 2–4. Loan exhibition gallery (as advertised): Monday to Saturday, 12–6.

Cambridge and County Folk Museum. Weekdays (Tuesday to Saturday, closed on Monday), 10.30–1, 2–5. Sundays and Bank Holidays, 2.30–4.30.

Classical Archaeology. Weekdays, 9–1, 2.15–5 (Saturdays, 9–1).

Archaeology and Ethnology (Downing Street). Weekdays, 2–4.

Geology (Sedgwick) (Downing Street). Weekdays, 9–5.

Whipple Museum of the History of Science (Free School Lane). Weekdays during term at times posted at Museum.

Scott Polar Research Institute. Weekdays, 2.30–4.

Botanic Garden. Winter, 8 (or dawn)–dusk; summer, 8–7.30 (plant houses 2–5). Open on Sundays to key-holders only.

LIBRARIES

City Public Library (Wheeler Street, back of Guildhall). Lending Library: Monday to Friday, 10–6; Saturday, 10–5. Reference Library: 9–9; Saturday, 9–5. Information Bureau and Box Office: Monday to Friday, 9–6; Saturday, 9–5. **Tourist information on Sundays** from June to September: 10.30–3.30.

University Library (Burrell's Walk or West Road). Open from 9 a.m.–10 p.m. during full term for readers only (Saturday, 9–1). Visitors must normally be accompanied by a graduate of the University but, by permission, small parties are conducted round by members of the staff at 3 on Monday to Friday. The Library is closed for some days at Easter, Christmas and in September.

Corpus Christi College Library. Open Monday to Friday, 2–4 (5 in summer).

Pepys Library (**Magdalene College**). Open to visitors during full term, and for some weeks in July and August, 11.30–12.30, 2.30–3.30 on weekdays.

St John's College Library. Visitors, 11–1 on weekdays in term.

Trinity College, Wren Library. Visitors: Monday–Friday, 2.15–4.45 (winter, 3.45); Saturday (full term only), 10.45–12.45.

Trinity Hall Library. Open Monday to Friday, 10.30–12.30 during full term. (Chained books.)

GENERAL

Tourist information is available from June to September from the kiosk in the Market Square, Monday to Saturday, 10–6.

Early closing. Most large stores are open six days a week, but some are closed all day on Monday. Some other shops are closed on Thursday or Saturday.

Cambridge Railway Station is one mile from the City centre. From London, there are services from both King's Cross and Liverpool Street. Train enquiries, telephone Cambridge 59711.

Cambridge Bus Station is in Drummer Street (through Bradwell's Court, St Andrew's Street). Bus enquiries, telephone Cambridge 53418.

Cambridge Airport (Marshall's) is at the junction of the New-market and Teversham roads. Passenger enquiries, telephone Cambridge 56291. (Flying School, telephone Cambridge 56291).

Addenbrooke's Hospital, Hills Road (Outpatient Department and Accident Service), telephone Cambridge 45151. (Addenbrooke's Hospital, Trumpington Street: Cambridge 55671.)

Boating. Boats may be hired for the Upper River (the Granta) at the bottom of Mill Lane; for the Lower River at Victoria Bridge, and for the Backs at Magdalene Bridge and Silver Street Bridge. On certain days in summer there are return river trips to Ely starting from Victoria Bridge. The University and College boathouses line the river on the north side opposite Midsummer Common, but the eight-oar races, etc., are rowed down the river.

Swimming. The Parkside Pool in Mill Road (at the eastern corner of Parker's Piece) has heated water and is open all the year. There are open-air pools (May to September) on Jesus Green and Cold-ham's Common, and public bathing-places at Sheeps Green.

Golf. The Gog Magog Golf Club course is on the Hills Road, about $3\frac{1}{2}$ miles from Cambridge (telephone Cambridge 47626).

Bowls. There are public greens on Christ's Pieces and Jesus Green. The Cambridge & County Bowling Club is in Brooklands Avenue (telephone Cambridge 53615).

Lawn Tennis. There are public courts on Christ's Pieces and Jesus Green (Park Parade end).

Newspapers and Journals
Cambridge Evening News, 4p.
Cambridge Independent Press & Chronicle (Thursdays), $3\frac{1}{2}$p.
Cambridge Review (twice each term), 25p.
Granta (occasionally during term)
University Reporter (Wednesdays during term and as required), 5p.

Theatres and Cinemas
A.D.C. Theatre, *Park Street*; Arts Theatre, *Peas Hill*
Arts Cinema, *Market Passage*; ABC 1 & 2, *St Andrew's Street*
Victoria 1 & 2, *Market Hill*

American Military Cemetery (see page 93) is open to visitors every day of the week: in summer, 8–6; in winter, 9–dusk.

Sports Grounds

University Athletics, *Milton Road*
University Bathing Sheds, *Grantchester Meadows*
University Cricket, Hockey, Lawn Tennis, *Fenners, Gresham Road*
University Football, *Grange Road*
University Lacrosse, *Grantchester Road*
University Real Tennis Courts, *Grange Road/Burrell's Walk*
City Football, *Milton Road*; United Football, *Newmarket Road*
City Rugby Football, *Grantchester Road*
Caius A.F.C., Cricket, Hockey, Lawn Tennis, *Barton Road*
Caius R.U.F.C., *Coton Footpath*
Christ's and Sidney Sussex, *Huntingdon Road*
Churchill, *at the College*
Clare, *approach by Bentley Road*; Tennis, *Grange Road*
Corpus Christi, *Cranmer Road*
Downing, *Long Road, off Hills Road*
Emmanuel, *Wilberforce Road*
Fitzwilliam, *Oxford Road*; A.F.C., *Grantchester Street*
Girton, *at the College*
Jesus, *on the Close, at the College*
King's and Selwyn, *Fulbrooke Road, off Grantchester Road*
King's Tennis, *West Road*
Magdalene, *Milton Road*
Newnham, *at the College*
Pembroke, *Grantchester Road*
Peterhouse, *Porson Road*
Queens', *Barton Road*
St Catharine's, *King's Road, Newnham*
St John's, *corner of Queen's and Madingley Roads*
Selwyn, *see King's*
Sidney Sussex, *see Christ's*
Trinity Cricket, etc., *corner of Adams Road*
Trinity Lawn Tennis and Hockey, *Cranmer Road*
Trinity Sports, *Grantchester Road*
Trinity Hall, *Huntingdon Road*

Aerial view of Cambridge, with King's College Chapel in the centre

Cambridge

The town planning of the older part of Cambridge is simple, and takes the form of the letter **Y**. *The arms of this* **Y** *are formed by two main thoroughfares meeting at the Round Church, from which the tail goes off to Huntingdon via Girton College. The arm nearer to the station consists of Hills Road, Regent Street, St Andrew's Street, Sidney Street and Bridge Street, all nearly in a straight line. The other arm, which begins as if it were going to run parallel but eventually curves and inclines, consists of Trumpington Road, Trumpington Street, King's Parade, Trinity Street and St John's Street, all continuous. These two main thoroughfares are connected northwards by* (1) *Lensfield Road,* (2) *Downing Street and Pembroke Street* (*one straight line*), (3) *Petty Cury and Market Hill, and* (4) *Market Street. The tail of the* **Y**, *past the Round Church, is formed by Bridge Street, Magdalene Street, Castle Street and Huntingdon Road.*

FROM the railway-station a 'bus (No. 101 service) can be taken to Emmanuel College. The 'bus route follows the Station Road, and at its end turns right into the Hills Road, which is the old Roman road running from the Gogmagog Hills through Cambridge to Huntingdon. Almost immediately after the corner into Hills Road has been turned, the visitor will see ahead on his left the Roman Catholic Church of Our Lady and the English Martyrs. Its spire, the highest in Cambridge, is 216 feet high, and the entire cost of its construction (completed 1890) was borne by Mrs Lyne-Stephens, wife of the famous art collector and the original 'Duvernay' (the dancer) of *The Ingoldsby Legends*. The chimes of this church are well worth hearing. It has a peal of eight bells with Angelus. The tenor weighs 32 cwt., and is by far the largest bell in the county.

Round the corner to the left, a few yards down Lensfield Road, is the **Scott Polar Research Institute,** a small domed building,

designed by Sir Herbert Baker, R.A., and opened in 1934. A
feature of the interior is the domes painted with maps of the
Arctic and Antarctic regions by Mr Macdonald Gill. On the
front of the building is a bust of Captain Scott, by Lady Hilton
Young (Lady Scott), with the inscription over—QUAESIVIT
ARCANA POLI VIDET DEI, 'He sought the secrets of the Pole, now
he sees (the secrets) of God.' In the forecourt is a bronze statue,
also by Lady Hilton Young.

Next to the Scott Polar Institute, and completely dwarfing it,
is the striking University Chemical Laboratory, designed by
J. Murray Easton and Howard Robertson, and opened in 1958.

Continuing in a straight line down Hills Road and the rather
dull Regent Street, the road changes its name to St Andrew's
Street. In it are three colleges, to which we shall return later. On
the left is the entrance to Downing College. On the other side of
the road we get the buildings of the University Arms Hotel and
a glimpse of the extensive common known as Parker's Piece.
A little further down St Andrew's Street the 'bus stops opposite
Emmanuel College (on the right), and further down still (also
on the right) is Christ's College. The visitor should walk on
past Christ's College and turn to the left down the narrow street
called Petty Cury.

At the other end of Petty Cury, keep to the side of the Market
Square (along the front of the Guildhall) and turn left along
Peas Hill into Bene't Street. The building on the left of this
street is the 'Arts School', but it has nothing to do with the
teaching of drawing and painting: it was put up in 1910 to
provide additional lecture rooms for the University. On the
ground floor are a lecture theatre accommodating 300 persons
and four large lecture rooms. The upper floors contain smaller
lecture rooms and class rooms.

Before leaving Bene't Street, the visitor should pause at the
corner of Free School Lane, so called because the local Grammar
School (the Perse School) originally stood here. Walking a few
paces down this lane, he will see old and new buildings in really
startling proximity. Almost opposite the rough rubble wall of
the arched covered passage which led the scholars of Corpus

Christi College directly to the church of St Benedict (Bene't), before the College had its own chapel, will be seen the famous Cavendish Laboratory; behind it are the Mond Laboratory (Physics) and the Museum of Zoology.

Returning to Bene't Street, the visitor should note the church of St Bene't, whose Saxon tower is the oldest building in Cambridge, and whose well-marked features—the belfry windows and plain lancets, the quoins of long-and-short work—will hold the attention of all interested in pre-Norman architecture.

Continuing down Bene't Street, we reach Trumpington Street, and turning to the left we soon find on the same side of the road **Corpus Christi College.** Its exterior is medieval only in appearance; the gateway, with its flanking turrets, and the entire first court are modern (1823–7). Northwards, to the left as we enter, is the Hall, and the passage in the far left-hand corner leads through to the Old Court.

Corpus Christi College was founded in 1352 by the two town guilds of Corpus Christi and the Blessed Virgin Mary, and is unique among the colleges in having a democratic origin. The low-pitched chambers of the old court are typical dwellings of the time of Edward the Third. All that was necessary to a college was contained in this earliest of quadrangles. Three sides were given to rooms for scholars; on the south side (from west to east) ran the Kitchen, the Buttery and Hall, and the Common Room, with the Master's Lodge and the Library over it. For chapel the scholars used the neighbouring church of St Bene't.

Undergraduates now 'keep' in the Lodge, as the Master has a new Lodge in the first court. The old Hall is now used as a kitchen and an eighteenth-century window has replaced its earlier oriel; but as a whole the appearance of the court must be much the same now as it was in the days of Elizabeth I. Even the buttresses added to strengthen the walls date from the Wars of the Roses. Look particularly at the ground-floor room on the right-hand side of R staircase. Here once lived the most brilliant of Shakespeare's contemporaries, the poet and dramatist Christopher Marlowe, to whose memory a tablet has been placed on the wall. Another famous Jacobean playwright, John Fletcher, was admitted to Corpus about the year of Marlowe's death (1593). Other worthies who were members of the College include Sir Nicholas Bacon, Keeper of the Great Seal to Elizabeth, and Archbishop Parker, a former Master, who bequeathed a priceless collection of manuscripts to the College. In addition to these treasures Corpus possesses probably the finest collection of old plate in Cambridge. The Library and Collection of Gems are open to the public and should be visited if time permit.*

Tennyson, the poet, when an undergraduate at Trinity, had rooms on the first floor of what was then 59 Trumpington Street. This house has since been altered and now forms part of Corpus.

In 1963–4 the College took an important step by adapting and enlarging Leckhampton House (on the other side of the river, in Grange Road, facing Selwyn College) to provide accommodation for graduate researchers, whose numbers had grown very rapidly in Cambridge during the previous ten to fifteen years.

Opposite Corpus, on the other side of Trumpington Street, stands the three-sided red-brick court of **St Catharine's**, which has a dignified eighteenth-century appearance. Pink chestnuts replace the grove of trees that for centuries screened it from the street. Newer buildings added to the north side bring this wing close to the pavement of Trumpington Street.

St Catharine's College was founded in 1473 by Dr Wodelarke, Provost of King's. The original buildings have entirely dis-appeared, and the College was practically rebuilt by Dr Eachard, Master in 1675–97, who died before the projected fourth side was completed. It was not till 1704 that the Chapel was built, during the mastership of the youthful Sir William Dawes, who was elected Vice-Chancellor of the University at the age of twenty-six. He lived to be Bishop of Chester and afterwards Archbishop of York, but his happiest days were spent in Cam-bridge before he lost his still more youthful wife, whose memory

* For times of opening, see page 13.

Corpus Christi College: the Old Court

St Catharine's College from Trumpington Street

is kept fresh by his touching inscription in the College Chapel. The whole Chapel is wainscoted, the reredos and organ gallery being particularly impressive.

New blocks have been added since 1930, and there is a new Combination Room,* built in 1932. The Master's Lodge, which faces the entrance to Queens' College, was designed by W. M. Fawcett and dates from 1875. Fawcett was one of the most prolific of Cambridge nineteenth-century architects.

By no means richly endowed at its foundation, St Catharine's had a windfall when Dr Gostlin, a Master of Caius, left it in 1626 the adjoining piece of land on which stood the famous Bull Inn, incorporated in the College in 1946. The Fellows of his own college were deeply mortified at losing this property, and Bishop Browne, in his history of St Catharine's, relates that for years there was an annual toast at Caius 'to the unhappy memory of Dr Gosling, who was such a goose as to leave the Bull to Catharine'.

Between the Bull and St Catharine's there formerly existed the George Inn, famous as the hostelry of the University carrier, Thomas Hobson, immortalised by Milton. His way of dealing with customers who came to his livery stables—they were compelled to take the horse nearest his hand, 'This or none'—is still remembered and celebrated as 'Hobson's Choice'.

Coming out of St Catharine's into Trumpington Street again, the visitor should turn to the right (southwards) and go up the street, passing Silver Street, till, on the opposite side, he sees the entrance to **Pembroke College,** now one of the largest colleges in the University. Architecturally, it is less imposing than many of the smaller colleges, but it has some features of unique interest. In the north-west corner of the first court is the original chapel, now used as a library. This dates from about 1355, and the moulded ceiling of 1690 and bookcases of the period add to the

---

* The Combination Room is the parlour to which the dons of a college retire after they have dined in Hall. Here they smoke, talk and drink their coffee. The term 'Combination Room' appears to be peculiar to Cambridge. All other universities call it the Senior Common Room.

Pembroke College Chapel

beauty of the interior. Sir Christopher Wren was the architect of the present Chapel, built in 1663–4 at the cost of his uncle, Dr Wren, then Bishop of Ely. Some original woodwork remains.

The College is rich in literary and historical associations. Spenser, the author of *The Faërie Queene*, was in residence from 1569 to 1576. Thomas Gray lived here from 1756 to 1771, and a college tradition maintains that after the poet's death the future statesman, William Pitt, occupied Gray's first-floor rooms in the Hitcham Building (in the Second Court) from 1773 to 1780. Among a number of renowned Pembroke divines were Archbishop Whitgift, of Canterbury, and Bishop Ridley, the martyr. South of the Master's Lodge is a path still called 'Ridley's Walk'.

Pembroke College was founded in 1346 by the Countess of Pembroke. The original court was diminutive (55 by 95 feet only), and, in addition to the Chapel, contained a Combination Room with Master's Lodge above in the opposite S.E. corner. The Hall, Kitchen and Buttery were on the east side, and chambers on the south and west. This Hall, Combination Room and Master's Lodge were razed to the ground in 1874 on the advice of the architect, Waterhouse, who designed a new Lodge in Pembroke Street, and in the same year the present Hall was begun. This Lodge is now used for college rooms, and another new Lodge, by Maurice Webb, was built in 1933 on part of the Fellows' Garden, in Tennis Court Road. In 1880 George Gilbert Scott junior lengthened Wren's Chapel. The remainder of the buildings, which extend far back along Pembroke Street, are modern, the Scott Building (1883) being followed by the New Court (1907, by Caröe) and the Orchard Building (1957–8) designed by Marshall Sisson. The last named has the arms of the college strikingly carved and coloured on one end. Of Gray's old college little now remains save the two chapels and the mid-seventeenth-century Second Court (1635–59).

The battlemented building opposite Pembroke, with a central tower and oriel window, was built by Blore in 1831–3 out of surplus money collected for a statue in London of William Pitt, and was placed here so as to be opposite Pitt's old college.

Until 1963 it was the headquarters of the University Press (the Pitt Press), which still has publishing offices and a showroom in the building. The actual printing was transferred to new premises in Shaftesbury Road (off Brooklands Avenue) in 1963.

In Mill Lane stands the attractive building of Stuart House (1925), designed by G. Hubbard and known to many outside Cambridge as the home of the Board of Extra-mural Studies. Between Mill Lane and Little St Mary's Lane, overlooking the river, is the **University Centre** by Howell, Killick, Partridge and Amis. Opened in 1967, the Centre provides dining and recreational facilities for members of the graduate staff of the University and registered research students.

Continuing southwards along Trumpington Street on our way from Pembroke to Peterhouse, we pass on our right Little St Mary's Lane, in which is the Museum of Classical Archaeology with its comprehensive collection of casts of ancient sculpture.

The great antiquity of Peterhouse will be best appreciated by a visitor who slips round the corner of Little St Mary's Lane and peeps over the churchyard of St Mary-the-Less at the venerable clunch exterior of the northern side of the college. Notice also the gallery connecting the college with this church, which until about 1650 was used as the chapel of Peterhouse. St Mary-the-Less dates from about 1350 and was built on the site of a twelfth-century church dedicated to St Peter, from which the college takes its name. A fragment of the tower of this earlier church still exists in the north-west angle. No citizen of the United States should fail to visit the interior of St Mary-the-Less, for it contains a tablet to the memory of the Rev. Godfrey Washington (1670–1729), a Fellow of Peterhouse; and over the tablet appear the family's armorial bearings, stars and stripes surmounted by an eagle. This monument was erected in 1736, and forty years later, in 1776, the national flag of the United States was borrowed —eagle and all—from the Washington coat-of-arms.

Just past the corner of Little St Mary's Lane, facing the main thoroughfare of Trumpington Street, stands **Peterhouse**, which has the distinction of being the earliest collegiate foundation in

Peterhouse: the Chapel and Burrough's Building

the University. The gabled building seen from the road, with its oriel window, and the Chapel in the centre of the court, date only from the time of Charles I, but some of the primitive thirteenth-century buildings remain. The original Hall, though altered, is still standing, and the doorways at either end of the passage (known as the 'screens') are unaltered.

An examination of Peterhouse will help the visitor to understand the gradual development of the now familiar planning of colleges in courts. When colleges began to be founded in the thirteenth century, the founders could provide only what was indispensable. The men must have rooms in which to sleep and work, a hall in which to have the common meal, and a consecrated building in which to pray. For the last of these the nearest church served, for the first of them one or two of the ordinary houses of the period would do, but the hall had to be built. So with Peterhouse the first buildings to be erected, about 1288, were the Hall and Buttery.*

Peterhouse (officially St Peter's College, but called that only in formal documents) was founded in 1284 by Hugh de Balsham, Bishop of Ely, whose original fourteen scholars with their Master were installed in two houses situated approximately where the north side of the present entrance court now stands. When the bishop died in 1286 he left his scholars 300 marks with which they bought a piece of land behind their houses and 'built thereon a handsome Hall'. Go right through the entrance court, pass through the screen, and compare the masonry of the Hall with that of the kitchen (1450) and surrounding buildings. This second court is really the first and earliest court. About 1424 a range of chambers for undergraduates was put up on the north side, and a few years later another range, containing the Library, was begun on the west side. In 1460 a third side was completed on the south by the building of the Combination Room (known as the 'Stone Parlour') with the Master's lodging over it. Thus was formed a three-sided court, the fourth (east) side being

*A Buttery is not a bar—though beer may be obtained there. It is both an office where the undergraduate gives his orders for food and drink and the store-room from which he gets his groceries.

Peterhouse: the William Stone Building

closed by a wall, between which and the street stood the two
original houses bought by Balsham. These two houses were
pulled down and replaced by a range of chambers during the
mastership (1625–34) of Dr Matthew Wren, uncle of the famous
architect Sir Christopher Wren. Dr Wren also began the building
of the delightful Chapel and Cloisters, though these were not
finished till after the Restoration. Most of the woodwork in the

Chapel is contemporary with the building and is most attractive. Meanwhile, an earlier master, Dr Perne, had bequeathed his library and a sum of money to the college in 1590, and Dr Wren made new accommodation for this bequest by extending the south wing of the old court, beyond the Combination Room, to the street. This projection now forms the left side of the entrance court as you enter the college; the building on the north side was erected in 1738–42. Later additions to the college buildings include Gisborne Court (1825–6), the Hostel (1926, by T. H. Lyon), Fen Court (1939, by Hughes and Bicknell), and lately the William Stone Building by Sir Leslie Martin and Colin Wilson in 1963–4. The Master's Lodge, a pleasant Queen Anne building, faces the College from the other side of Trumpington Street. It was built as a private house in 1701 and given to the College in 1727.

After leaving Peterhouse, the visitor should turn to the right and walk a little further along Trumpington Street to see the **Fitzwilliam Museum,** whose Corinthian portico appears on the same side of the road as Peterhouse. If he does not go in at once there are so many other things to see in Cambridge that he will be in danger of leaving the University with its art treasures unvisited.

The Fitzwilliam is one of the oldest public museums in Great Britain. It contains the University's art collections and is among the outstanding museums of Europe. It was founded by Richard, 7th Viscount Fitzwilliam of Merrion, in 1816 when he bequeathed to the University, in which he took his M.A. degree in 1764, his fine art collections, his library, and the sum of £100,000 to provide 'a good substantial convenient Museum Repository or other building'. Included in the Founder's bequest were 144 paintings, among them a Titian, a Veronese, and a Rembrandt; a series of Rembrandt's etchings which was then regarded as the finest in England; and excellent collections of the work of many other important engravers. Lord Fitzwilliam's library included 130 medieval illuminated manuscripts and an outstanding collection of music autographs.

The building of the Museum was begun in 1837 to the designs of George Basevi, and it ranks highly in the architecture of the period. Basevi died in 1845 and C. R. Cockerell was appointed to complete the unfinished interior, but funds ran out and the Entrance Hall was not completed until the year 1875 under the direction of E. M. Barry. Meanwhile the Founder's collection (which since 1816 had been exhibited elsewhere in Cambridge), augmented by gifts and bequests to the University of antiquities, paintings and other works of art, was moved into the building and opened to the public in 1848.

During the 150 years which have elapsed since its foundation the Museum has grown to its present stature by the generosity of many private benefactors; in this century special mention must be made of Charles Brinsley Marlay, Sir William Courtauld, Captain William Newsam McClean, James Stewart Henderson and John Charrington (all of Trinity College), of Miss Sydney Renée Courtauld (Newnham College) and Sir Stephen Courtauld (King's College), and of W. Graham Robertson. Their bene-factions have more than doubled the extent of the Museum building and have greatly enhanced its collections. Additional reserve areas were opened in 1966.

The chief collections comprise Egyptian, Greek and Roman antiquities, coins and medals, medieval manuscripts, paintings and drawings, prints, pottery and porcelain, textiles, arms and armour, medieval and Renaissance objects of art, and the Library, which includes the music collection and literary autographs.

The Egyptian and West Asiatic Department covers a period from remote prehistoric times down to the Christian era. There are numerous examples of the various classes of grave-furniture, reliefs and sculpture.

The Greek and Roman Department includes a collection of vases from the earliest times down to the fourth century B.C., bronzes, sculpture, jewellery, glass, and objects of domestic use.

The Coin Room houses a collection which is the most important in this country after that in the British Museum, amounting to about 100,000 coins, medals and seals. The coins range from examples of the earliest known coinage to that of the present

The Fitzwilliam Museum

time, and include a very fine Greek collection. Admission is for students only.

The Department of Paintings and Drawings is extensive and includes examples of the Italian, Flemish, Dutch, French, British and Spanish schools, covering a period from the Middle Ages to the present day. Most representative are the Italian, Dutch and English collections, which provide a good general illustration of the history and development of these schools. The paintings are supplemented by a collection of Old Master drawings and of British water-colours, together with English portrait miniatures.

The Print Room is noteworthy for its splendid collection of portraits, especially French of the seventeenth century, and

The Fitzwilliam Museum: part of the Greek gallery

English of the eighteenth century. The main strength of the rest of the collection lies in its seventeenth-century prints, particularly of the Dutch school, but the German engravers of the sixteenth century and the French of the eighteenth century are also well represented.

The *Pottery and Porcelain* is among the foremost of English ceramic collections, surpassed only by those in the British Museum and the Victoria and Albert Museum. Most important, on account of its wealth and completeness, is the English pottery; but English porcelain, and Chinese, Near Eastern and Continental pottery and porcelain, are also represented by numerous and excellent examples, and in some sections they are of outstanding importance. Accompanying the Oriental Collection are fine Chinese jades and bronzes.

The Department of Textiles includes the best existing collection of English samplers and many good foreign ones, embroideries from the Greek islands and Near East, and noble examples of Italian and Turkish cut velvets.

The *Arms and Armour* consist of examples mainly of the sixteenth and seventeenth centuries, though a few pieces of the Gothic epoch are included.

The Collection of Applied Art also includes a small but fine group of carved ivories (Coptic, Byzantine, Carolingian and medieval), excellent examples of medieval and Renaissance enamel work, and fine pieces of Elizabethan and other silver.

The Library contains about 25,000 volumes, of which over 15,000 are modern books relating to the arts, and a collection of early printed books. The music collection, consisting of both manuscript and printed music, is one of the best in England, and is remarkable especially for the autograph compositions it contains, of which the most noteworthy are those by English and Italian composers and by G. F. Handel. The important collection of medieval and later manuscripts totals over 800 items, including manuscript cuttings and some oriental manuscripts. Mainly remarkable for their artistic interest, many of the manuscripts are of the finest quality. The Library also includes a collection of literary autographs. (Admission on application to the Librarian.)

Opposite the Museum is an old house, bearing on the front its
date, 1727. From 1893 to 1963 this was known as Fitzwilliam
House and was the headquarters of the Non-Collegiate members
of the University. (See Fitzwilliam College, p. 70.)

On the same side as the former Fitzwilliam House, but further
south along the Trumpington Road, is the old building of
Addenbrooke's Hospital (see page 84). After leaving the Fitzwilliam Museum, however, the visitor whose main concern is
with the colleges should go back to the corner of Silver Street and
turn left down this till, in the first road to the right (Queens'
Lane), he sees the entrance to **Queens' College.**

Queens' is the first college we reach with a bridge and river
frontage. It is with Queens' that the world-famous 'Backs' begin.
More ambitious in its planning than Peterhouse or Corpus, the
first court, all in red brick, with its square corner-turrets and
entrance gateway flanked by towers, is pure fifteenth-century
workmanship. Passing straight through the Hall screen we enter
the Cloister Court, which is one of the most attractive courts in
Cambridge. Begun about 1460, it has a brick cloister on three
sides. The northern cloister is overhung by the picturesque
half-timbered Gallery of the President's Lodge, built about
1540, and panelled inside about the end of the same century. The
Hall and Combination Room of the Old Court form the east side
of this quadrangle. The President's front door is in the north-
west corner. These two courts together are a model of the early
Tudor manor house, and the arrangement is the same as that of
Haddon Hall.

Queens' College was founded in 1447 by Andrew Dokett, who
secured Queen Margaret of Anjou as his patroness. When the
Lancastrian dynasty fell with Henry VI, the College fortunately
obtained the patronage of Elizabeth Woodville, wife of Edward
IV, who refounded it in 1465. Hence in writing the name of the
Cambridge College we must be careful to put the apostrophe
after the 's', in memory of the two queens concerned in its
foundation. On the north side of the Old Court are the Library
(west) and the Old Chapel (east), now used as a lecture room

Queens' College: the President's Lodge in Cloister Court

Queens' College: the Mathematical Bridge

and library annexe. Between them, under the old sun-dial and
modern clock-tower, is an arched passage leading to Walnut
Tree Court. This consists of the other side of the Old Chapel and
a range of dignified Jacobean chambers bearing on the street
front the date 1618. The third side is formed by the new chapel
(1891), and beyond this is Friars' Court with buildings of 1886
and 1912. Its fourth side (the Erasmus Building), along the river
bank, was completed in 1960 from designs by Sir Basil Spence.
Skirting the lawn which has always held a walnut tree, and
retiring from the modern chapel along the wall that hides the
delightful garden of the President, we can return by a passage
in the south-west corner to the Cloister Court. Keeping straight
along by the Hall we must cross the south Cloister to reach the
diminutive Pump Court, containing a block of chambers erected
by James Essex in 1756. The turret between this and the Old
Court is known as the Erasmus Tower, because it was in these
rooms that the great Dutch scholar lived (1510–13) when he
came to Cambridge as Professor of Greek.

   From the Cloister Court an archway in the centre of the west
wing leads to the unique wooden bridge crossing the Cam. The
original bridge, which dated from 1749, was rebuilt in 1867. Go
over it and turn right along the river front. Opposite you is the
Lodge of Queens', but from further along you will have some
beautiful views of King's College. Behind you is the Fisher
Court of Queens', a large curvilinear block built in 1936 to the
design of G. C. Drinkwater, to commemorate the four-hundredth
anniversary of the death of John Fisher, President of the College
from 1505 to 1508. At its eastern end it is flanked by a charmingly
reconstructed seventeenth-century brewhouse, which serves as
an undergraduates' common room.

   On leaving Fisher Court turn to the right along Silver Street.
On your left is **Darwin College**, founded in 1964 by Gonville
and Caius, St John's and Trinity Colleges as 'a place of education,
learning and research' for graduate students in Cambridge. Part
of the College is situated in the former Newnham Grange, the
home of the Darwin family since 1873 (Gwen Raverat, author of

Darwin College: rear view from a branch of the River Cam

Selwyn College from Grange Road

Period Piece, lived here as a girl). Membership of the College, including its Fellowships, is open to both men and women.

Now go straight ahead and up Sidgwick Avenue. At the first corner on the left-hand side is **Ridley Hall**, opened in 1881 as a theological college for graduates of any university who intend to take Holy Orders in the Church of England. The original buildings were designed by C. S. Luck, the chapel (1891–2) by W. Wallace, and its reredos (1949) by Sir Albert Richardson. Go past the front of Ridley Hall, turn right, and you will see the main entrance to Newnham College for women.

Newnham College, opened in 1875, was designed throughout by Basil Champneys. The bronze entrance gates were presented in memory of Miss Clough, the first Principal of the College (1875–92), by students who had resided at Newnham during her headship. The eastern part, which we see on entering, was built in 1893, and is known by the name of its donors as the Pfeiffer Building; it is connected by corridors with the Old Hall (south) and with Sidgwick Hall (north). Beyond this is the large Clough Hall, and between this and Sidgwick Hall is the entrance to the handsome library given to the college in 1897 by Mr and Mrs Henry Yates Thompson. The range west of Clough Hall is Kennedy Buildings, built in 1905, and at right angles to this wing is Peile Hall, built in 1910. The Fawcett Building, designed by Elizabeth Scott and running alongside Sidgwick Avenue, was added in 1938. A new gatehouse, opening the College towards Sidgwick Avenue, was added in 1949, from designs by Buckland and Heywood. The Principal's Lodge, designed by Louis Osmond, dates from 1957–8. Planned like a classical villa, with a central court, it startles the visitor with the sheets of plate glass, used from floor to roof, with which this courtyard is walled all round. The glass is variegated with abstract patterns symbolising the four seasons. These were designed by Geoffrey Clarke, who planned the windows in the new cathedral at Coventry. An extension to the college library, designed by Christophe Grillet, was added in 1961–2. The Strachey Building, also by Grillet,

Newnham College: Clough Hall

was opened in 1968 to house undergraduates and Fellows; it is named after a former Principal of the College.

Going back to Sidgwick Avenue, and turning left into it, we see the red brick buildings of Selwyn College on the right at the corner of Grange Road. On our way there we pass a large block of University lecture rooms and libraries, begun in 1958, some by Sir Hugh Casson and Neville Conder, others by James Stirling.

Selwyn College was founded in 1882 in memory of George Augustus Selwyn, the first Bishop of New Zealand. Religious tests in the existing colleges—all previously Anglican—had recently been abolished, and Selwyn was founded to compensate for this. Membership was therefore restricted to baptised Christians; and all Fellows, Scholars, and Exhibitioners had also to be Anglicans. The necessary money was speedily raised from subscribers who approved of these principles. The limitation of membership to Christians was, however, abandoned during the second quarter of the twentieth century; and in 1957 new statutes abolished the restriction of Fellowships, Scholarships, and Exhibitions to Anglicans. The lofty Tudor Gothic Chapel was designed by Sir Arthur Blomfield. The Hall, which has some fine eighteenth-century woodwork taken from an old English church in Rotterdam, was built in 1908–9 from designs by Grayson and Ould. The Library, of two stories, connected to the college by an arch with a passage over, is by T. H. Lyon.

Leaving Selwyn, turn right along Grange Road. In a few yards you pass, on the other side of the road, a big new Selwyn court (by Cartwright, Woollatt and Partners) begun in 1967. Turn first right into West Road. Near the far end, right, is Harvey Court (1962) by Sir Leslie Martin and Colin Wilson. Part of Caius College, but standing several hundred yards away from the main buildings, it is unlike any other court in Cambridge in its layout.

Almost facing the lower end of West Road, a little to the left, is the iron gateway, embellished with painted heraldic shields,

King's College: the Gatehouse and Chapel

King's College: the Chapel and Fellows' Building

which forms the back entrance to **King's College.** The path
from the gate to the bridge over the river is bright in early spring
with masses of aconites and crocuses and later with daffodils.
The bridge was built in 1818. Pause on it to take in the views on
either side. To your right (south) is a charming scene with the
grove and wooden bridge of Queens'; on the left (northwards) is
Clare College with its bridge, and further on the bridges of
Garret Hostel and Trinity. Passing over the bridge you come
upon the great lawn of King's, and the Chapel is in front of you.
Its foundation stone was laid in 1446 by Henry VI, founder of
the College, but many years and several kings passed away before
its completion. Despite the civil warfare of the period, however,
work was spasmodically continued during the reigns of Edward
IV, Richard III, and Henry VII, till it was completed in the
sixth year (1515) of Henry VIII. The tale of its slow growth is
unfolded by the different kinds of stone used for its walls, the
white limestone marking the earliest part built by Henry VI.
Despite the long years which brought changes in architectural
ideals, the Gothic merging into the Renaissance style, the main
original design was adhered to throughout and the Chapel has all
the splendour of variety enshrined in unity. It is generally
regarded as the finest example of Perpendicular architecture in
England. It is world-famous for the early sixteenth-century
coloured glass in its vast area of window space, for its wonderful
stone roof with its fan tracery, and for the magnificent organ-
screen of Italian workmanship erected when Anne Boleyn was
Queen, and bearing her initials A. R. and the Boleyn arms with
those of England. The organ case dates from 1688, and has earlier
portions. A huge painting by Rubens, 'The Adoration of the
Magi', was presented to the College in 1961 and has been placed
behind the high altar.

King's Chapel is no less renowned for the exquisite music of
its services. Orlando Gibbons was among its choristers, and
today its choir is world-famous through the broadcasting each
Christmas Eve of the Service of Nine Lessons and Carols.
Nobody visiting Cambridge during term should miss hearing
a service there.

King's College Chapel: the Organ

King's is closely connected with Eton College, and the arms of the two are the same. Henry VI, the founder of both, obtained special privileges for his College from the University and until the middle of the nineteenth century only Etonians were eligible as Scholars or Fellows of King's. In 1851 the College abandoned its special privileges.

King's College, despite the venerable and impressive aspect of

King's College: Market Hostel, Peas Hill

its exterior, is, in its actual buildings, apart from the Chapel, comparatively modern. The Fellows' Building, facing the entrance gate and on our right as we leave the Chapel, dates from 1724. All the rest is nineteenth-century work. The Hall (reached by turning to the left at the end of Fellows' Building) was built by Wilkins in 1824 on the model of Crosby Hall, London, and the Library and Provost's Lodge (on our left going back towards the bridge) date from the same year. The fountain, surmounted by a

Great St Mary's Church from the Old Schools

statue of Henry VI, in the first court, was designed in 1879 by
H. H. Armstead. The Chetwynd Building (which borders King's
Parade) of 1870 is by Sir George Gilbert Scott. Market Hostel
in Peas Hill (by Architects' Co-partnership) was built in 1960-2.
In 1965 a joint scheme with St Catharine's College was started.
Designed by Sir James Cubitt and Partners on a large site
extending on both sides of King's Lane, it includes rooms for
undergraduates, kitchens and a small concert hall.

A way out of King's can be found by a small iron gate on the farther side of the Chapel; this way out has the advantage of allowing the visitor to see the old tower-gateway (right), which in ancient times was the entrance to an old court of King's, long disappeared.

But it will probably be found better to leave King's by the main entrance, which brings us out into King's Parade, one of the principal thoroughfares of the city. This is a continuation of Trumpington Street, down which we have already walked, and if we turn to the right on coming out of King's it will bring us back to Corpus and St Catharine's. We should turn to the left, therefore, on leaving the college, and go north.

On our right is **Great St Mary's** (a parish church and the University church) in which the University Sermon is preached on some Sunday afternoons in term time. A good specimen of late Perpendicular work, it has features of interest to the antiquary, particularly the tower begun in 1491 and completed in 1608, and the Jacobean font (1632); but its characteristic most familiar to undergraduates and townsfolk was the curfew, which rang nightly from 9 to 9.15 until the war of 1939 began.

Behind Great St Mary's is the square where the market is held on Saturdays. This is known as Market Hill. Strangers who note how level it is may ask, 'Why *hill*?' The answer is that the name dates back many centuries, to a time when the surrounding land was a swamp and had not been built up to its present level.

A new wing of Caius College, designed by J. Murray Easton, was built on the north side of Market Hill in 1934. At the other end of Market Hill is the big Guildhall, largely rebuilt to the designs of C. Cowles-Voysey and reopened in 1938.

Facing the west front of Great St Mary's are the Old Schools and the Senate House. The Old Schools stand back from the street, behind Senate House Green. They are the former lecture rooms of the medieval University, their age being concealed by a front added in 1754–61. Long used for housing the University Library, they reverted in 1934 to their original use for lectures, University committees and other functions, and are beautifully decorated and furnished. The more modern buildings to the

Candidates arriving at the Senate House to receive their degrees

Gonville and Caius College: Caius Court

north and west were also formerly part of the University Library
and are now used for administrative offices and departmental
libraries.

The Senate House, at right-angles to the Old Schools, dates
from 1730, and was designed by James Gibbs. This is the
parliament house of the University, where its senior members
meet on Congregation days to legislate and where degrees are
conferred by the Chancellor or Vice-Chancellor. The ceremonies
used on these occasions date back to the Middle Ages. Visitors
are admitted.

As we walk down King's Parade from King's College we shall
have noticed ahead of us on our left a high corner building. This
is part of **Gonville and Caius College,** but if we want to see
the most picturesque part of this ancient foundation we should
turn sharply to the left down Senate House Passage and make
our entrance by the old Gate of Honour on our right. The main
entrance to the College is in Trinity Street (a continuation of
King's Parade) and is modern; formerly the site was occupied by
a narrow doorway called the Gate of Humility. Through this
portal arrived the medieval schoolboy and walked along a shaded
path (now flanked by rooms) till he arrived at a second and more
resplendent archway, the Gate of Virtue, which still stands.
Through this he passed to take up his residence in the room
allotted to him, and leading the virtuous life on which he had
entered he ultimately passed out of the College by the Gate of
Honour to take his degree at the Senate House. Founded by a
doctor, Caius has always had a large number of men reading
medicine for their degree, and among those who once passed
through the Gate of Honour was the great William Harvey,
who discovered the circulation of the blood.

Caius (pronounced 'Keys') College, more properly Gonville
and Caius, was founded in 1348 by Edmund Gonville, and
refounded by Dr Caius in 1557. Entering by the Gate of Honour
we come into Caius Court, which the good doctor added to the
original foundation. On the east is the Gate of Virtue (also
designed by Caius, who had a passion for symbolism) and

opposite (to the north) is the old Gonville Court. As we go
through the passage we should look inside Gonville's Chapel
(right), built in 1393, and containing the remarkable tomb of
Dr Caius put up in 1575, only two years after his death, by
Theodore Haveus of Cleves; on the left a door in the passage
admits to the Master's Lodge, dating from 1441. About the
same time were built the Old Hall (now used as a Library), the
old Library (now a Combination Room) and the chambers on
the west and south. The east wing was built about fifty years later.
The great antiquity of Gonville Court is to some extent obscured,
however, by the classical facing given it in 1753. The new Hall
(1853), approached by a vestibule out of Gonville Court, contains
portraits of many famous Caius men in addition to the founder:
among them Jeremy Taylor, Thomas Gresham, founder of the
Royal Exchange, Dr Swete, the divine, and J. R. Seeley, the
historian. Returning to Caius Court, we pass through the Gate
of Virtue into Tree Court (rebuilt by Waterhouse in 1870), and
so out by the modern gateway into Trinity Street. Facing this
gate, on the other side of the street, is St Michael's Court, by
Aston Webb (1903).

By whichever gate we leave Caius it will be simplest to go
straight down Senate House Passage again (away from King's
Parade) as far as we can go, when we shall find ourselves facing
Trinity Hall. This ancient College should not be confused with
Trinity College, from which it is entirely separate and distinct.
'The Hall', as it is affectionately called, is a small college,
but it has a great reputation for law and rowing. It was for many
years Head of the River, and i's prowess in sport has not dimini-
shed its lustre for learning. A long list might be compiled of the
Lords Justices it has given to England, and other celebrities it
can claim are Bishop Gardiner, the poet Herrick, the novelist
Bulwer-Lytton, and Lord Chesterfield.
 Trinity Hall was founded by William Bateman, Bishop of
Norwich, in 1350, and now has three courts. The hall and
adjoining western and northern ranges of the principal (or first)
court were built by the founder, or shortly after his death, but

D

Trinity Hall: the Library

Clare College from across the river

they were much altered in the eighteenth century and a large part of this court was destroyed by fire in 1850. A great part is therefore modern and the College as a whole has a Georgian rather than a medieval appearance. The hall faces the entrance, and opposite its door is the Library, which is of the greatest architectural interest. It dates from the reign of Queen Elizabeth I and, still possessing its original reading desks and ancient arrangements of shelves and chained books, gives the best idea of a medieval library that can be obtained in Cambridge. The Fellows' Garden, with its terrace overlooking the river, contains some splendid chestnut trees, said to be over 200 years old. Later additions to the buildings include work by Sir Giles Gilbert Scott (1934), Sir Albert Richardson (1951) and Trevor Dannatt (1965). Trinity Hall has one of the best collections of plate in Cambridge, including the Founder's Cup, given before the year 1352.

On leaving Trinity Hall by the gateway through which we entered, we turn sharply to the right and a few steps bring us to the handsome iron gate (1714) of its neighbour, **Clare College.** This is one of the most beautiful of all the colleges, and has the appearance of a Jacobean palace rather than a seat of learning. Though the College is the second oldest foundation in Cambridge, the buildings we now see were begun in 1638, and the first court was not finished till 1715. There is a tradition that Inigo Jones was responsible for these buildings, but there is no evidence to support this.

Clare College has the unique distinction of having been originally founded by the University itself in 1326 as University Hall. It was refounded by Lady Elizabeth de Clare as Clare Hall in 1338, not being renamed Clare College until as recently as 1856.* The original buildings fell to ruin in the sixteenth century and the College was completely rebuilt during the next century. The Chapel (north-east corner) was built about fifty

* The name 'Clare Hall' was revived by being given to a new college (for graduates of either sex) founded by the Master and Fellows of Clare College in 1965. Its premises are in Herschel Road.

years after the rest of the first Court had been finished and
contains an 'Annunciation' by Cipriani over the altar. In the
centre of the northern range (to our right) is a flight of steps
leading to the Hall, and beyond this, over the Kitchens, are the
Combination Room and Library, the latter containing some
early seventeenth-century bookcases and many other objects of
interest.

Pass straight through the College to visit the gardens and the
famous bridge of Clare. This, built in 1640, is one of the sights
of Cambridge. Observe the stone balls which decorate its top,
but make no rash bet as to the exact number of them. A slice
has been cut out of the last one on the left-hand (southern) side.

After lingering on Clare Bridge to enjoy the views of the river,
pass on through another gate of handsome ironwork. Facing
you on the opposite side of the road is the new court of Clare,
designed by Sir Giles Gilbert Scott as a war memorial to members
of the College and opened in 1934. In the centre of a frontage of
300 feet is an archway 80 feet high leading to the court. Within
the archway is a roll of honour. The trust deed requires an
annual ceremony in the Memorial Court on Armistice Day.

Behind this is the new **University Library,** opened in 1934
by King George V. Built to the imposing design of Sir Giles
Gilbert Scott, this magnificent addition to the University
buildings was made possible by the munificence of the Inter-
national Education Board (founded by Mr John D. Rockefeller,
jun.), by the generous contributions of past Cambridge men,
and by the sacrifices made by King's and Clare Colleges in giving
up their playing field on the site. The Library can be approached
from the Backs (Queen's Road) either on foot by Burrell's Walk
or through the Clare extension, or by car from West Road (see
map); but the best view of the building as a whole is probably
the one from Grange Road (parallel to the Backs), when the
great tower, which is a feature of the design, can be seen in rela-
tion to the rest of the Library.

Like the British Museum and the Bodleian at Oxford, the
Library is entitled to a copy of every book published in Great

The University Library

Britain, and the new building contains many miles of steel shelves holding very many thousands of volumes directly accessible to the reader. Among its principal treasures are the famous manuscripts of the Gospels known as the Codex Bezae, the only perfect copy of Caxton's *Golden Legend*, and the rarest of all printed books, the Gutenberg Bible, which dates from about 1450. An outstanding feature of the interior is the great Reading Room, a magnificent apartment nearly 200 feet long; and as a result of the architect's skill all the principal rooms are not only stately in their proportions, but exceptionally well lighted.

Returning to the Backs, recross the river by the graceful Garret Hostel Bridge, named from an old hostel that is now part of Trinity. The old bridge was constructed in 1837. The new bridge was built in 1959–60 from designs by Guy Morgan and his son Timothy, who was an undergraduate at the time and died in the year that the bridge was completed.

Keep straight on after crossing the bridge, and Garret Hostel Lane and (left) Trinity Lane will bring you back into Trinity Street. When you reach it, turn to your left and in a hundred yards you will be rewarded by a sight of the Great Gate of **Trinity College,** with its two archways for large and little doors, its statue of Henry VIII (the founder), and below this the arms of Edward III (centre) and his six sons. The arms of the Black Prince, immediately to the left of the centre, will easily be recognised by the three ostrich feathers on either side and the motto *Ich dien.* The blank shield to the left stands for little Prince William, who died in infancy. The west front of the gate, rather later in style, has statues of James I, his Queen, and Prince Charles.

The Great Court of Trinity is the largest college court in the world. The eye will be caught immediately by the beautiful Renaissance fountain which a famous Master of the College, Thomas Nevile, had built in 1602. It is not really in the exact centre, and part of the fascination of Trinity lies in its harmonious irregularity. No two sides of the Great Court are alike, and no two meet at right-angles. These peculiarities, together with the three gateways that ornament the court, are the result of the royal founder having rolled three colleges into one to create his new foundation.

As we enter the Great Court we face the west wing, which contains the Master's Lodge (right) and the College Hall (centre). On our left is the fine Queen's Gate, with a statue of Elizabeth I, built in 1597. On our right is the Chapel, and farther along the

Trinity College: Great Court, showing the Chapel and Fountain

Trinity College: the Wren Library from across the river

same side is the still more ancient King Edward's Gate. Before the reign of Henry VIII this belonged to the old King's Hall, and when built in 1427 it was the first four-turreted gateway in Cambridge. It used to stand about where the sun-dial is now and was removed to its present position by Thomas Nevile, who built the Queen's Gate as a pendant.

Trinity College, founded in 1546, absorbed three older institutions: King's Hall, Michaelhouse and Physwick Hostel. The largest was King's Hall, founded in 1336 by Edward III. It occupied a square running back approximately from a line between the sun-dial and the Great Gate past King Edward's Gate. Behind this last, northwards and facing the Bowling Green, is a row of chambers that formed part of King's Hall. Michaelhouse, founded by Edward the Second's Chancellor, Hervey de Stanton, in 1323, was situated in the south-west of the Great Court. Parts of it exist in chambers next to Trinity Lane, and the walls of its Hall are retained in the present butteries and Old Combination Room. On the south side of the court were the houses of Physwick Hostel, which originally belonged to Caius. The Great Gate was begun in 1518 by the Master of King's Hall, but only half finished in 1535. Apart from this and King Edward's Gate and the Chapel (completed about 1564) and a few fragments here and there, all that we see of the Great Court of Trinity is due to the genius of Dr Nevile, Master from 1593 to 1615. He found his College a confused mass of ill-assorted and, in some instances, tumbledown buildings, destitute of planning and order. A row of buildings ran out from the east side to near the centre of the present court: another row projected inwards from the west almost opposite the Great Gate. He cleared away the projecting chambers, continued the east side to meet the row of old houses on the south, rebuilt the Hall more or less on the Michaelhouse site, shifted back the venerable King Edward's Gate into line with the Chapel, and extended this north side to meet a corresponding extension of the southern. Nor did his grandiose schemes stop here; he not only gave the College its fountain, but also defrayed the whole expense of building behind the Hall the beautiful court that bears his name.

Before we move on from the Great Gate, let us look at E staircase near by. Among the many famous men who once had rooms on this staircase (first to the right) are Sir Isaac Newton, Lord Macaulay and Thackeray. Statues of the two first, and also of Bacon and Tennyson, will be found in the Chapel, which should next be visited. The famous statue of Newton, by Roubiliac, inspired Wordsworth's lines about

> The antechapel where the statue stood
> Of Newton, with his prism and silent face,
> The marble index of a mind for ever
> Voyaging through strange seas of thought alone.

The fine early eighteenth-century woodwork should be noticed, also the nineteenth-century windows and wall paintings. After leaving the Chapel, keep on the same side till you have examined King Edward's Gate, then take the nearest path to look at the Fountain and afterwards cross by another path to visit the Hall in the centre of the west side. Big as this Hall is, the College is so much bigger that the undergraduates have to dine in relays, less than a third of their total number being able to sit down at a time.

As you go up the steps to enter the Hall, turn round for a last view of the big court—it is one of the best—and admire the Renaissance portal through which you pass. People familiar with the hall of the Middle Temple in London will quickly see that the Hall of Trinity College is similar, both in size and style. Notice the Jacobean woodwork and also the portraits of Henry VIII by Holbein, of the little Duke of Gloucester by Reynolds, of the famous scholar Bentley by Hudson, and of Tennyson by G. F. Watts.

Coming out of the Hall, do not return to the Great Court, but continue through the 'screens' or passage-way and pass out of the other door down the steps into Nevile's Court. Or, better still, pause a moment on the balustraded terrace to admire the beauty of this cloistered court and the noble arches of the Library opposite you. This splendid building, designed (without a fee) by Sir Christopher Wren, was a later addition to the cloisters, which in Nevile's time were bounded on the west by a

wall. In designing this library, Wren deliberately entered into
competition with his great Italian predecessor, Sansovino, and
the Library of Trinity may bear comparison with that of St
Mark's at Venice. A door in the north-west corner of the cloisters
admits to the no less sumptuous interior. The effect of the noble
proportions and airy lighting is enhanced by the beautifully
carved bookcases made under Wren's own supervision. Grinling
Gibbons, the foremost craftsman of his day, and never yet
surpassed, was responsible for the carved wreaths of fruit and
flowers. A splendid series of marble busts by Roubiliac and other
sculptors gives a final touch of dignity to the Library and
honours the memory of Trinity celebrities. At the southern end
is Thorwaldsen's statue of Byron, which was declined by St
Paul's and Westminster Abbey and left to languish for years in
the cellars of the Custom House in London till Dr Whewell got
to hear of it and gave it an honoured resting place in the poet's
own college.

On leaving the Library, walk under it to the far end, turn left,
then right into New Court, designed by Wilkins in 1823–5.
The smaller but attractive Bishop's Hostel, designed by Robert
Minchin (a carpenter) in 1671, lies next to it, to the east. Leaving
New Court by the exit opposite to Bishop's Hostel, we walk
along an avenue of trees and soon come to the fine three-arched
Trinity Bridge, built by Essex in 1765. The avenue from the
bridge to the back gate (given to the College in 1733) was
replanted in 1949.

We cross Trinity Bridge and take the path to the right leading
us over a small iron footbridge into the grounds of **St John's
College.** In some ways, it would be preferable to lead the visitor
through this College from the front gate, so that he might view
the buildings in chronological order; but since this guide has
been compiled with the primary object of saving time, it is
proposed, with one digression, to go from the back to the front.

St John's College occupies the site of the still more ancient
Hospital of St John, which was established in 1135. This institution, largely by reason of internal dissensions, had fallen into

Boating on the Backs by Trinity Bridge

St John's College: the Bridge of Sighs

St John's College: the Gatehouse

decay by the beginning of the sixteenth century, and after the
death of Henry VII in 1509 his mother, Lady Margaret Beaufort,
Countess of Richmond, obtained permission to convert the
hospital into a college of the University. The memory of the
foundress is kept ever fresh by the oarsmen of the College, who
call themselves 'The Lady Margaret Boat Club'. Originally the
College had one court only, the first, of which the gateway and
north side are contemporary with the foundress. The south side

was rebuilt in 1772. The second court dates from about 1607, the Library was thrown out towards the river in 1623–8, and the rest of the third court built in 1671.

The grounds of St John's are most pleasant and extensive. It is not considered 'correct' to admire the tall 'New Buildings' (1831) which flank the northern edge of the lawns; yet, seen from the distance between the trees, this open cloister surmounted by pinnacles and minarets is decidedly attractive. Skirting this nineteenth-century building, we should recross the river by the beautiful stone bridge of three arches built from Wren's design in 1709–12. As we go over we note to our left the high covered bridge built in 1826 and called 'The Bridge of Sighs', after the famous bridge of that name that links the Doge's Palace to the prison in Venice. Apart from the name there are few points of resemblance in the two bridges.

In front of us, after we have crossed the old bridge, is an early eighteenth-century gateway with two piers, each surmounted by an eagle, the crest of St John's. Do *not* pass through this gateway, but before you reach it turn sharply to the left through a little passage that brings you into the Third Court of the College. Note the handsome Renaissance gateway in the centre of the side to your left as you enter; also the date, 1671, which may be observed on the river side of the building. If we cross the court diagonally, an archway in the eastern side, which was originally the back gate of the College, leads us to the Second Court, a beautiful example of Elizabethan brickwork (1598–1602). Walk straight across this court to the archway opposite.   By this time the experienced visitor will recognise the darkened passage beyond as the familiar 'screens', and will expect to find the Hall on his left and the kitchens on his right.

Opposite the kitchen is the spacious Hall with its original open roof, an old lofty screen at the back, and several interesting portraits. The portrait of himself by Samuel Butler, author of *Erewhon*, Romney's portrait of Noah Thomas, Rigaud's Matthew Prior, and Pickersgill's Wordsworth are especially to be noted. More remains behind. Walk up to the high table, pass out (*but only with permission*) by the door on the left, and go up the

stairs to the long Gallery or Combination Room. With its
panelled walls and richly moulded ceiling it is one of the finest
apartments of its kind in England. It leads us to the Library,
another fine example of Jacobean Gothic, built in 1623–8, which
illustrates a new development of library-designing in the bookcases attached now to the side walls. The founder of the Library
was John Williams, Bishop of Lincoln, keeper of the Great Seal;
hence the letters, cut in stone on the end of the building overlooking the river, which often puzzle visitors: I L C S , standing for
Johannes Lincolniensis Custos Sigilli.

We can return either by the way we came or by a fine seventeenth-century staircase that leads down into the Second Court.

Whichever route is chosen we have still to see the First Court
on the other side of the Hall. Architecturally it is not so good as
the Second. Its best feature is the very early sixteenth-century
east side, with its noble four-turreted gateway, certainly one of
the three finest in Cambridge and thought by several good
authorities to be the most beautiful of any. The square-towered
Chapel was designed by Sir George Gilbert Scott and built in
1864. Its interior contains little of antiquarian interest save the
monument of Hugh Ashton, an ecclesiastic of Lady Margaret's
household, whose canopied tomb was removed here from the
original chapel pulled down in 1869. St John's Chapel is celebrated for its musical services.

The west door of the Chapel opens on to Chapel Court. The
older part of this dates from 1885, the remainder (by Sir Edward
Maufe) from 1938–9.

The new Cripps Building, by Powell and Moya, was begun in
1964 between New Court and Magdalene College, to accommodate
about 200 members of the College. It spans the Bin Brook and is
fringed by a lake at a point near to where the brook joins the
river. The lake is used as a punt harbour.

As the visitor emerges from the College and comes into the
road, let him turn to look back at the richly ornamented gate,
with its sculptured antelopes supporting the coat of arms on
a background spangled with marguerites in memory of the
foundress. The statue of St John the Evangelist dates from 1662,

replacing one that had been removed by the Puritans during the Civil War.

Opposite the gate of St John's an open space marks the site of the church of All Saints, demolished in 1865. Its graveyard has a stone cross to the memory of Henry Kirke White (1785–1806), the poet and hymn-writer, of St John's College. Along one side of All Saints' Passage, and stretching from Trinity Street to Sidney Street, is a detached part of Trinity College (Whewell's Court), designed by Salvin and built during the years 1859–68.

We are now in St John's Street, a continuation of Trinity Street. If we turn to the left on coming out of St John's, we shall pass on our right the modern red-brick University lecture rooms called the Divinity School (by Champneys, 1879). At the end of the street we are brought to a stop before the Church of the Holy Sepulchre, one of the four round churches in England. The interior of this church retains its main twelfth-century features unaltered and is still an exquisite building. The rect-angular chancel and north aisle were added in the fourteenth century. In 1842 the church was restored by the Cambridge Camden Society and the restorers overdid their work. Behind the church is the Cambridge Union Society, the largest University club, famous for its debates, in which many Cabinet Ministers have had their first training in public speaking.

From the Round Church we should go north down Bridge Street, and cross the river by the 'Great Bridge'. This un-attractive iron structure of 1823 occupies the site of a medieval bridge.

As we go across we see on our right the river front of **Magdalene College.** Crossing the bridge, we enter the College by the main gateway a few yards down the street on the right.

Though rather out of the way, Magdalene has so many titles to distinction that it should not be overlooked. It has always been a small college, but has produced many eminent scholars. Its worthies include characters so different as Charles Kingsley, Charles Stewart Parnell and Arthur Christopher Benson. It is famous above all for its connection with the diarist, Samuel Pepys, who bequeathed his remarkable collection of books and engravings to his old College. This collection is now contained in the handsome Pepys Library in the Second Court, and its most precious treasure is the original manuscript of the donor's famous Diary. Pepys began his Diary in January 1660 and closed it, owing to failing eyesight, in May 1669.

Magdalene College was founded in 1542 by Thomas Lord Audley on the site of the older Buckingham College, a hostel for Benedictine monks dating from the reign of Henry VI. Parts of the older buildings still exist. Entering the College by the present gateway, which was built in 1585, we find the Hall and Chapel opposite us on the north side. Both belonged to Buckingham College, though the old chapel was lengthened and restored in the middle of the nineteenth century. The Hall was originally built for the Benedictines in 1519 by the Duke of Buckingham. The present wainscoting dates from 1714. Note here the portrait of Pepys by Sir Peter Lely. Coming out of the Hall turn to the left and enter the Second Court. Before you is a beautiful seventeenth-century building with the inscription BIBLIOTHECA PEPYSIANA 1724. This date commemorates the year when the Pepys bequest was received, the building itself having been erected at least thirty years earlier. Here are not only the diarist's books, but also a dozen old oak bookcases which Pepys used in his own house. The Library is shown to visitors at certain hours: enquiries about these should be made at the Porter's Lodge.

Various new buildings were erected to face the river and Magdalene Street early in the twentieth century. In 1925 the College began to expand across Magdalene Street, where a number of timber-framed medieval houses were converted into the charmingly informal Mallory Court. A new block by Lutyens, dating from 1932, stands close to these adapted buildings, stretching down to the river, and forms a striking contrast.

Just over the crossroads beyond Magdalene is the **Cambridge and County Folk Museum** (at 2 Castle Street, formerly an inn known as the White Horse). Opened in 1936, the Museum's

Magdalene College: the Pepys Library

Magdalene College: Mallory Court

Churchill College: a courtyard in one of the residential blocks

aim is to interest Cambridgeshire people in the social life of
their ancestors during the past few hundred years, and to preserve
articles of daily use that are disappearing owing to changed social
conditions.

In Northampton Street (first on the left after Magdalene) are
two renovated cottages (nos. 17 and 18) occupied by **Lucy
Cavendish College** for women graduates. (Lucy Cavendish,
the widow of Lord Frederick Cavendish who was murdered in
Dublin in 1882, devoted much of her time to the education of
women.) The College derives from a society formed in 1951 by
women members of the Regent House who were not Fellows of
the existing colleges; it was recognised by the University in
1965. Its special concern is to help older women whose careers
have been interrupted, to fit themselves to return to academic or
other professional life.

Right, at the junction of Madingley Road with Northampton
Street, is **Westminster College.** Founded in London in 1844,
and transferred to Cambridge in 1899, it trains graduates of any
university for the Presbyterian ministry. The buildings are by
H. T. Hare. The Chapel contains some interesting modern
glasswork designed by Douglas Strachan. (Since 1967 Westminster has accommodated **Cheshunt College:** see p. 83.)

Farther along Madingley Road, at its junction with Storey's
Way, is **Churchill College,** the most recent collegiate foundation
in the University. This is the national memorial to Sir Winston
Churchill. The first turf was cut by Sir Winston in the autumn
of 1959, and the foundation stone was laid by the Chancellor of
the University in 1961. Buildings, designed by Richard Sheppard,
were begun very soon afterwards, and include common rooms,
dining hall, kitchens, the Master's Lodge, three residential
blocks, and a library block containing the Brendan Bracken
Reading Room, the Bevin Library and the Wolfson Hall. The
College is intended primarily for men reading for degrees in
science, and for the promotion of postgraduate studies.

A little farther along the Madingley Road are the
Observatories. The original Observatory was completed in
1824; the Solar Physics Observatory was brought to Cambridge
from South Kensington in 1913. The Observatories have been
almost entirely re-equipped during recent years and are well
provided with modern telescopes and other apparatus for
astronomical research.

Another excursion that can best be made from this end of the
town is to Girton College. Girton is outside Cambridge, along
the Huntingdon Road, which is a continuation of Magdalene
Street and Castle Street in a north-westerly direction.

At the crossroads formed by Magdalene Street, Northampton
Street and Chesterton Lane, note the church of St Giles, which
preserves in its south aisle the Norman chancel arch (*circa* 1070)
of the ancient church replaced by the new building (1875).
Almost opposite this is the tiny church of St Peter—ancient,
though partially rebuilt in 1781. The south door and the old
font, with its grotesque sculpture, are Norman. From these
crossroads the route is up Castle Street, which has a mound
(right) marking the site of the Castle erected by William the
Conqueror in 1068. The Castle, chiefly used as a prison, fell into
decay in the fifteenth century, and was finally abandoned and
dismantled in 1647. The Castle mound is open to visitors and
from it there is a fine view of the city and the country as far as
Ely Cathedral. The entrance to it lies in front of the Shire Hall
(1932), designed by H. H. Dunn. Castle Street continues as the
main Huntingdon Road.

A little farther along, on the left, is **New Hall,** founded in
1954 as a college for women members of the University. For its
first ten years they lived in 'The Hermitage' at the corner
of Silver Street and Queen's Road. They moved into the new
buildings (designed by Chamberlin, Powell and Bon) in 1964.
The buildings so far completed include the rectangular Library
with a barrel roof, the domed Hall, and a number of bed-sitting
rooms for undergraduates. Between the Hall and the Library is a
cool sunken courtyard with a fountain.

New Hall: the dome of the Dining Hall from the south-west

Just beyond New Hall, on the same side of the road, is
Fitzwilliam College. Fitzwilliam men are lineal descendants
of the Non-Collegiate students who were (in modern times) first
admitted to the University in 1869, thus reverting to the practice
of the medieval university before any colleges were founded in it.
From 1893 they had their headquarters in an old house facing
the Fitzwilliam Museum and hence called Fitzwilliam Hall (later
Fitzwilliam House). In 1963 they moved into the new buildings,
which were designed by Denys Lasdun. The Dining Hall, which
is very striking, has a white vault of concrete and glass. Fitzwilliam
achieved full collegiate status in 1966.

Half a mile or more further on, on the right-hand side of the
road, is the National Institute of Agricultural Botany, opened in
1921 by King George V. It is a fine building, designed by
P. Morley Horder. A little further on is Girton College.

Girton College owes its origin to no one wealthy donor, but
to the movement for the higher education of women during the
1860's. It began modestly in a house at Hitchin in 1869, but two
years later further funds were raised, sixteen acres were bought
at Girton, and in 1873 the present buildings were begun, the
architect being Alfred Waterhouse. Since then it has rapidly
expanded. The College now has accommodation for 180 students
and is well equipped with Hall, Chapel, Library, lecture rooms,
laboratories, and a swimming-bath, while the grounds alone
cover 33 acres. The Chapel has a noteworthy coloured window,
by L. C. Evetts, inserted in 1955.

The visitor who wishes to reserve Girton for a special ex-
cursion should turn left on leaving Magdalene, recross the bridge
by the way he came, and continue straight on, past the Round
Church, till he comes to the first road on the left, Jesus Lane.
Turning down Jesus Lane we see, on the left, the University
Pitt Club, founded in 1835. Just past it, on the left, is Park
Street, in which is situated the theatre of the Amateur Dramatic
Club, built in 1935 on the site of an older theatre. Cambridge's
first multi-storey car park is appropriately also in Park Street.

Fitzwilliam College

Girton College

Returning to Jesus Lane and continuing eastwards, we soon
reach (on the left) **Wesley House**, a theological college of the
Methodist Church, opened in 1930. The Chapel, on the east side
of the court, contains decorative paintings by Harold Speed;
and the buildings, in red brick and Ancaster stone, also include
the Principal's residence, Hall, common rooms and accommodation for residents. Sir Aston Webb and Son were the architects.

On the opposite side of Jesus Lane, a few yards further on,
is **Westcott House**, a post-graduate theological college of the
Church of England. The buildings that stand round its pleasant
court are of various dates from 1899 to 1926, the Chapel and
Library being by P. Morley Horder. Immediately beyond
Westcott House is the parish church of All Saints, built by
G. F. Bodley in 1864. It has a fine tower and spire and contains
the font from the destroyed church of All Saints in the Jewry.

Facing All Saints is the entrance to **Jesus College**. The
College incorporates the buildings of the Benedictine nunnery
of St Radegund, founded soon after the year 1130, and differs
from all other colleges in being monastic in plan. The walled
path leading from the street to the gate-tower is commonly
called 'The Chimney'. It has the Master's garden behind the
right-hand wall as you go in and the Fellows' garden on the left.
Jesus College was founded in 1496 (when the nunnery was
suppressed) by the Bishop of Ely, John Alcock, whose badge, a
cock standing on a globe, is a pun on his name. It will be seen
on the entrance gate and on many other parts of the College
buildings. The distinctive gate-tower of the College is unlike any
other. It was built by Alcock. Immediately you have gone under
it, bear towards the right and go through the founder's archway
into the Cloister. The Hall, which stands on the north side of
the Cloister, was the nuns' refectory.* The balustered gallery of
the Hall was added in 1962, when the upper part of the west
wall was demolished and the oriel window which it contained

* The Hall is reached by the left-hand door immediately inside the
founder's archway with the motto *Prosperum iter facias*.

Jesus College: entrance gateway and 'Chimney'

was rebuilt in the farther wall. The gallery opens into the Upper
Hall, which has an attractive open-timbered roof dating from
the early sixteenth century. The thirteenth-century arches on the
east side of the Cloister were the entrance to the Chapter House.
The Chapel on the south side was the church of the nunnery.
Its earliest part is the north transept, which is Norman. The rest
of the Chapel is Transitional Norman or Early English. Some of

Jesus College: North Court

Sidney Sussex College: the Chapel

the woodwork, including the end of the Master's stall with its charming effigy of Alcock, dates from the founder's time. The rest (including the screen) is by Pugin, who restored the Chapel in 1848–9. The glass in the eastern lancet windows is by Pugin and in the large Perpendicular windows by Burne-Jones. The painting on the nave roof is from designs by William Morris.

The beautiful Old Library, which is not normally open to visitors, dates from the foundation of the College. The other buildings are of various dates. The 1930 range in Chapel Court was designed by P. Morley Horder. Over one of the arches is a coat of arms, with supporting angels, carved by Eric Gill. The North Court (1965) was designed by David Roberts.

Jesus stands in the most spacious grounds of any college in the University. Thomas Cranmer was at the College, as under-graduate and Fellow, for a quarter of a century. Laurence Sterne, the author of *Tristram Shandy*, was also a Jesus man, as was Samuel Taylor Coleridge, the poet. Sir Arthur Quiller-Couch ('Q') was a Fellow of the College from 1912 until his death in 1944, during which time he was Professor of English.

From Jesus we must turn back down Jesus Lane, and soon we see on our left the boundary wall of **Sidney Sussex College.** Follow this wall and it will lead to the entrance of the College in Sidney Street. The Hall should be visited, if only to see the contemporary portrait of Oliver Cromwell, who entered this college as a Fellow-Commoner on the day that Shakespeare died, 23rd April 1616.

Sidney Sussex College was founded in 1589 by Lady Francis Sidney of Penshurst, Countess of Sussex, on the site of a religious house previously occupied by Franciscan friars. The northern court was completed in 1598, and contained the Hall and (on the first floor) the Master's Lodge above the Buttery and Kitchen. The southern court was built in 1628; but the old red brick of these courts was obscured and the general appearance of the College changed during the nineteenth century, when much of the exterior was cemented and a new gateway built. A vanished relic of the Franciscans was the old refectory (on the east side of the second court), which was fitted up as a chapel in 1602. The Chapel was rebuilt by Essex in 1776–82 and in 1912 extensively enlarged by T. H. Lyon. It has an elaborate marble pavement and oak-panelled walls. A distinctive feature is the arcaded annexe leading to the little side-chapel on the west side erected in memory of Bishop Hicks. The Chapel is a gem of modern work and should not be missed. A court with a cloister was built by S. L. Pearson in 1890. There has been further building since. This includes a range along Sussex Street (1938–9) designed by E. R. Barrow, with shops on the ground floor on the street side; and a still later range (1967–9) by Howell, Killick, Partridge and Amis at the junction of King Street and Malcolm Street.

Coming out of Sidney we turn to the left and go up Sidney Street, passing Market Street on our right, and keep straight on till we come to the corner of Petty Cury (right). Facing this street is **Christ's College** (left), the college of Milton. If possible we should time our visit to be between 2 and 4 p.m., when the historic garden is open to the public. There we may see the shored-up mulberry tree which tradition associates with Milton, who resided from 1625 to 1632.

Christ's College, like St John's, was founded by the Lady Margaret, Countess of Richmond, who absorbed in her new College an older institution called God's House, which a devout parson, William Bingham, had founded about 1442. Note how the gateway resembles that of St John's. As we enter the principal court from the street, the rooms Milton is said to have occupied are on our left. His windows are on the first floor between the first staircase and the gate. Owing to the perishing of the original material (clunch) the whole of this court and the street front were repaired and given a classical appearance during the eighteenth century. The Chapel, on the north side, contains some fine fragments of old stained glass obtained from the former God's House in 1510, but the interior decorations generally are eighteenth-century and later. The brass eagle lectern dates from the late fifteenth century. The Master's Lodge, on the east side, has one precious relic of the past, an old

Christ's College: the Master's Lodge

stone fireplace decorated with Lady Margaret's arms, which belongs to the time of the foundress. The Hall, also on the east side, was largely rebuilt in 1876, but the old roof, though raised six feet, and the two windows looking into the Hall from the Master's Lodge, were retained.

Passing through the passage by the Hall in the south-east corner we come into the second court. Facing us is the noble Fellows' Building of 1640-3, of which tradition says (wrongly) that Inigo Jones was the architect. In the centre of this building is an iron gate which admits to the beautiful garden, with its famous mulberry tree. The Third Court was begun from plans by J. J. Stevenson in 1888, and extended in 1905. Two new blocks were added by Sir Albert Richardson in 1948–53. He also added the lantern to the Stevenson building.

Returning to St Andrew's Street from Christ's we turn to the left and keep on until we come to the front of **Emmanuel College.** Entering the First Court, we find the Chapel, designed by Sir Christopher Wren in 1668, before us, but the general appearance of this court, owing to rebuilding, is eighteenth-century. On our left (north) is the Hall, and beyond this is a smaller court containing the Library.

Emmanuel College was founded in 1584 by the Puritan Sir Walter Mildmay and, like Sidney, is built on the ruins of an older religious house, which had belonged to the Dominicans in the thirteenth century. The founder adapted the existing buildings to suit his purpose, and turned the old Friary Church into his Hall, while the old Refectory (now the Library) was converted into a Chapel, though it ran north and south, and not east and west, as chapels normally do. The present entrance and the western and southern sides of the First Court were rebuilt during the eighteenth century. The eastern side with the cloister and chapel belongs to Wren's time, so that only the northern side, with the Hall, contains any part of the Dominican buildings.

Passing through the southern end of the cloister we come out past the Brick Building of 1634 into the charming grounds with a lake and running water. Many will agree that its series of gardens is one of the best features of Emmanuel. The College has grown much of recent years: a new court, connected with the older part by a tunnel under the street, was added to the north, on the other side of Emmanuel Street, in 1910–14. Towards the end of the nineteenth century a large hostel was built beyond the lake and an elaborate block of lecture rooms on the south-west. A second Hall and new kitchens, designed by Robert Hurd, were built at the corner of St Andrew's Street and Emmanuel Street in

Emmanuel College: the Chapel by Wren

Emmanuel College: the Garden

Downing College

1957–9, a new Master's Lodge by Tom Hancock in 1963–4, and
residential accommodation (also by Hancock) in 1966.

Visitors from the United States will hardly need reminding
that John Harvard, who founded the famous university in the
New World, was an Emmanuel man. A tablet to his memory
was placed by members of Harvard University in 1904 in the
Chapel of Emmanuel, which also contains a stained-glass window
commemorating John Harvard among the series of windows put
in to mark the College tercentenary in 1884.

Coming out of Emmanuel by the main entrance again, turn to
the left up St Andrew's Street, pass Downing Street (right), and
a little further on, just after passing the opening into the big
public space known as Parker's Piece (left), cross the road and
go through the iron gates seen on the right. This is the entrance
to **Downing College,** so ambitious in its planning that had its
great court ever been completed its extent would have rivalled
that of Trinity. It is still incomplete, but the appearance and
accommodation of the College were greatly improved by the
construction of the handsome buildings forming the third side.

Downing College was founded by Sir George Downing. When
Sir George, a childless widower, died in 1749, he left his immense
fortune to his cousin Jacob, with the proviso that, should Sir
Jacob die heirless, the fortune should go to the endowment and
erection of a college at Cambridge. All possible heirs had pre-
deceased Sir Jacob when he died in 1764, and after considerable
litigation it was only in 1800 that the charter to found Downing
College was obtained. In 1807 the architect, Wilkins, began the
ambitious buildings, and the east and west sides were completed.
The Master's Lodge is the building with a portico on the east;
the building opposite it on the west side is the Hall. Four new
blocks of rooms on the north side (by Sir Herbert Baker, R.A.,
an Honorary Fellow of the College), together with some wrought
iron gates in memory of Professor Courtney Kenny, were formally
opened in 1932 by the Lord Chancellor, who is the Visitor of the
College. The north side was completed in 1956, when the fine
Chapel, designed by A. T. Scott, was consecrated. The altar

F

The University Botanic Garden

cross and candlesticks were designed by R. Y. Goodden and made by Leslie Durbin. In 1963 coloured glass windows by L. C. Evetts were inserted in the apse.

Until the early years of the present century an avenue of lime trees ran from what should have been the northern entrance to the College right through to Downing Street; but great portions of the grounds have now been built over, and the lime-tree walks with their graceful iron gates in Downing Street have been replaced by science museums and laboratories.

When Downing has been seen the visitor will have completed his survey of the colleges of the University, but he is far from having exhausted all the scholastic and educational institutions of Cambridge. Nobody interested in modern science should willingly miss at least a glimpse of the remarkable group of science museums and laboratories reached after leaving Downing by walking along Downing Street, which faces Emmanuel College. Most famous of them is the Cavendish Laboratory, the birthplace of the science of atomic physics.

Tennis Court Road links Downing Street with Lensfield Road. At the corner of Lensfield Road and Trumpington Road the visitor should note the old stone conduit, 'Hobson's Conduit', removed here in 1855 from Market Hill, where legend says it was erected in 1614. Almost opposite this corner is the **Leys School,** a public school for boys, established in 1875. The older buildings were designed by Robert Curwen, and the gateway and library by Sir Aston Webb were opened by King George V in 1914. Additional buildings have been erected in recent years.

Further south, along Bateman Street, are the very attractive buildings designed by P. Morley Horder and opened in 1915 for the use of Cheshunt College. The College, which prepares men chiefly for the Congregational ministry, has since 1967 been accommodated within the walls of Westminster College (see p. 67). The old Cheshunt College buildings have been sold.

Opposite Cheshunt College, on the other side of Bateman Street, is an entrance to the **University Botanic Garden.** This covers more than forty acres and has an attractive frontage along Trumpington Road, where there is another entrance with a pair of fine iron gates taken from the old Botanic Garden in Downing Street. A third entrance is in Hills Road, near the end of Station Road. The Garden exists primarily to provide for botanical teaching and research in the University.

Some other institutions should be mentioned, none of which is on any of the routes given. The first is **St Edmund's House,** situated on the north side of the city between the medieval centre and the newer colleges. The property was the gift of a former Duke of Norfolk, and for many years served as a House of Residence for Roman Catholic priests studying in the University. In 1965 St Edmund's became an Approved Society within the University, and it can now act as a college for graduates, including research students and senior visiting scholars.

University College was founded by the University in 1966 for Fellows and graduate researchers of either sex. Its present premises are at Bredon House, Selwyn Gardens.

Hughes Hall was founded as the Cambridge Training College for Women in 1885, and renamed in 1949. This is in Wollaston Road, overlooking 'Fenners', the famous University cricket ground. Its work is to train women graduates to become teachers in secondary schools.

Homerton College is situated on the Hills Road, about a quarter of a mile from Station Road corner. It occupies the buildings of Cavendish College, founded in 1876, which aimed at providing a university education for men younger and poorer than those at the other colleges. The experiment failed in 1891, and in 1894 the buildings were bought by the Congregational Board of Education, which transferred its Training College to them from Homerton in north-east London. This undenominational college offers a two-year course for women teachers in nursery, primary and secondary schools, and also specialist and post-graduate courses. The trustees of the College have added considerably to the buildings and amenities.

The **Perse School for Boys,** some distance further along the Hills Road, was founded in 1615 by Dr Perse, a Fellow of Caius. Originally in Free School Lane, it moved in 1890 to a site opposite the Roman Catholic Church, and from there to its present site in 1959. The architect of the new school was Stirrat Johnson-Marshall.

Further along Hills Road, at its junction with Worts Causeway, is the new **Addenbrooke's Hospital,** the first buildings of which were opened by the Queen in May 1962. It will be some time before the whole work of the hospital is transferred from the old building in Trumpington Street to this new site.

The Round Church (St Sepulchre's)

Some Cambridge Churches

All Saints. Of the old church, nothing remains but the font, preserved in the new church. The site, adjoining the Divinity School, is marked by a memorial cross. As this district between Sidney Street and Trinity Street was formerly inhabited by Jews, the church was known as All Saints in the Jewry. The new church of All Saints, designed by Bodley, was built opposite the entrance to Jesus College in 1864. (See p. 72.)

St Andrew the Great, opposite Christ's College, was destroyed and rebuilt in 1842. It is of interest as containing a memorial to Captain Cook, whose widow is buried in the nave.

St Andrew the Less, some distance from collegiate Cambridge, down the Newmarket Road, is usually called 'the Abbey Church', from its former connection with Barnwell Priory. The church is a typical example of early thirteenth-century (Early English) style, with a low side-window (fourteenth-century) and traces of a rood loft. Close to the church is a vaulted building of the thirteenth century, which, with a few fragments in the grounds of 'the Abbey House', is all that remains of **Barnwell Priory.** Further down the Newmarket Road is the interesting little chapel of **Stourbridge Hospital** of St Mary Magdalene, built in the twelfth century for lepers.

St Benedict (or Bene't) lies beside Corpus Christi College, of which it was formerly the chapel, being connected to the college by a gallery built about 1500. It is the oldest building in Cambridge, being of pre-Conquest date. The tower is typically 'Saxon', with its windows divided by baluster shafts, and the massive tower-arch, with roughly carved monsters, is impressive. In the south aisle is a brass to a former Chancellor of the University (1432), and near the entrance is the parish 'fire-hook' formerly used for pulling down burning houses. (See p. 19.)

St Botolph, adjoining Corpus Christi College on the south, is mainly of the fifteenth century. The chief points of interest are the chapel on the south, with early woodwork, and the picturesque font and cover, of the seventeenth century.

St Clement, in Bridge Street, contains work of various periods from the thirteenth to the sixteenth century and a brick chancel of about 1726. A spire, erected in 1821 through a bequest by William Cole, the antiquary, whose punning motto DEUM COLE appears on the west face of the tower, has been removed as unsafe.

St Edward's Passage, with the pinnacles of King's
College Chapel in the background

St Edward, King and Martyr, on Peas Hill, is almost
entirely of the fifteenth century. The two chapels on either side
of the chancel were built by the colleges of Clare and Trinity
Hall for the use of their members.

St Giles, in Castle Street, was probably the mother-church
of Cambridge, the old town being on the hill to the north of the
river. It was destroyed in 1875, but the chancel arch (of about

1070) and the nave doorway (twelfth century) have been built into the new church, where the early font is also preserved. (See p. 68.)

St Mary-the-Great, in the Market Square, is a Parish Church and also the University Church. The present church was begun in 1478, though the sedilia in the chancel probably belong to the earlier building of about 1350. The upper storey of the tower was not completed until 1608. The stone font is interesting as being dated 1632, and there are some oak benches of about the same date, while the galleries are good examples of their period (1735). (See p. 46.)

St Mary-the-Less was formerly dedicated to St Peter and gave its name to the adjoining college of Peterhouse, which used it as a chapel. Almost the whole of the present building dates from about 1350 and it is a good example of the Decorated style of that period. There is a late fifteenth-century brass of a man in doctor's academical dress, and Americans will be interested to note a tablet with the name and arms of the family of Washington. (See p. 25.)

St Michael, opposite Caius College, was connected with the extinct college of Michaelhouse, afterwards absorbed into Trinity College. It dates from 1327 and is in plan a simple rectangle, enclosing a collegiate choir, of which the stalls are fifteenth-century.

St Peter, in Castle Street, contains a carved Norman font. It is served from St Giles's Church opposite and is open daily. (See p. 68.)

St Sepulchre's is one of the four existing round churches in England. Built about 1130, it was enlarged in the fourteenth century, to which date the chancel and north aisle belong. In 1842 it was drastically restored. (See p. 63.)

Holy Trinity, at the corner of Market Street, has a tower of the late thirteenth century with internal buttresses. The nave and transepts are typical of the later Perpendicular period. On the north wall is a consecration cross. The celebrated Evangelical, Charles Simeon, was Vicar from 1783 to 1836.

The May Races

Excursions from Cambridge

The River

No serious rowing will be seen on that part of the river that
flows past the Backs of the Colleges. The 'business end' is
further down, beyond Jesus College, where the river becomes
much wider.

Go straight down Jesus Lane and after passing the College
turn left along the side of Midsummer Common and keep on
under the pleasant avenue of chestnut trees till you reach Victoria
Bridge, easily seen from the distance. A leisurely walk along the
bank eastwards, without crossing the bridge, will give a view of

Rupert Brooke writing in the garden of the Old Vicarage,
Grantchester, in 1911

The American Military Cemetery

the University and College boathouses. The Lent and May races are rowed much further down the river, beginning at Baitsbite, three miles away, and finishing at Old Chesterton, about a mile below Victoria Bridge.

From Victoria Bridge, on some days in summer, a motor-boat makes the trip to Ely (sixteen miles) and back. This cruise takes the visitor over the course of the races and shows him the well-known Ditton Corner and the best parts of the lower river.

Grantchester and Byron's Pool

For beauty of scenery and magic of association it is the upper river, known as the Granta,* that the visitor should make every endeavour to see. If he would explore this afloat, he should go to Silver Street, by Queens' College, and take a tiny turning to the left just before the Anchor Inn, and he will come out beyond the floodgate. There are several places on either bank where punts, canoes or skiffs are obtainable. He will then go *up* the river, past the City and University bathing sheds, till within an hour's easy pulling he arrives at the picturesque village of Grantchester.

This village is of great antiquity: it is mentioned by the Venerable Bede. The pool and mill are said to be the scene of Tennyson's 'Miller's Daughter', and its literary associations, which began with Chaucer, have continued through the centuries and were notably revived by the poetry of Rupert Brooke. The mill was, unfortunately, burnt down in 1928 and has not been rebuilt.

The pedestrian going to Grantchester should also make for Silver Street, cross the bridge, and then take the first turning to the left. Keep straight on till you come into Newnham Road, and then, when the road forks, bear to the left (avoiding Barton Road). This will bring you to a footpath leading across the fields to Grantchester.

* 'Granta' is the original name of the river. 'Cam' was a name derived, somewhere about 1600, from the name of the town by people who had forgotten its origin: 'Grantabridge', hardened into 'Cantabridge', which in turn was softened into Cambridge.

When you have reached Grantchester, afoot or afloat, go on to see Byron's Pool. This is more easily reached by road if the water is shallow, as it is likely to be in summer. Take the road past the disused mill, now a dwelling house only, leaving it on your right hand, and keep straight on till you come to a bridge over the river. Cross the bridge, turn to the right, just past a row of cottages, through a wicket gate; cross a small field and pass through another smaller gate. You are now in Trumpington and somewhere hereabouts stood Chaucer's famous mill. Follow a path through a pretty woodland glade until the pool is reached. This is called by Byron's name, but it was known to his prede-cessors and beloved by his successors. It has been a constant source of joy and inspiration to the noble army of poets that Cambridge has given to the world, from Chaucer and Spenser, Herrick, Milton, Marvell and Dryden, to Wordsworth, Coleridge, Tennyson, Fitzgerald and Rupert Brooke, who stayed at the Orchard at Grantchester in 1909–10 and later at the Old Vicarage, which he took as the title for one of his most famous poems.

Further Afield

No visitor to Cambridge should fail to visit **Ely.** The distance from Cambridge is about sixteen miles to the north-east. For those without cars there are frequent buses and a good rail service. From Ely journeys may be continued to Norwich, Lincoln and Peterborough. It is quite impossible in these pages to give details of Ely: these may be found in the local guides. But nowhere better can one find specimens of so many different styles of architecture—Norman, Early English, Decorated, Perpendicular, with some post-Reformation work, all in one building. Special attention may be given to the great west tower, which dominates the fens, from whichever way approached; to the octagon (Alan de Walsingham, 1342); the Galilee porch; the twelve-bay Norman nave; St Catherine's Chapel; the Prior's doorway, and the Lady Chapel (Decorated). Above all, view the exterior from the Broad Street entrance. Within the precincts are the gateway of Ely Porta and Prior Crauden's Chapel (now part of the King's School).

About four miles to the west of Cambridge lies the picturesque village of **Madingley**, which is reached by taking a turning to the right off the main road leading to St Neots and Bedford. Shortly after leaving the main road one passes the **American Military Cemetery** established in December 1943. It is in a beautiful situation and the hill behind it commands a fine view of the towers and spires of Cambridge, with the Gogmagog Hills behind and Ely Cathedral about fourteen miles away to the north.

Ely Cathedral by night

A folding map of Cambridge
follows this page: